AN
EYE
FOR
AN
I

AN EYE FOR AN I

RXTSA

POEMS BY HARRIET ZINNES

with drawings by:
Margit Beck, Nell Blaine,
Elias Friedensohn, Robert Rauschenberg,
Hyde Solomon and Theodore Stamos

FOLDER EDITIONS — NEW YORK

Some of the poems in this collection have appeared in the following publications: The A‍y‍ford Review, Canadian Forum, Chelsea, Epos, Mademoiselle, A New Folder: Americans: Po and Drawings, The New York Times, Penny Poems from Midwestern University, The Po Review, Poetry Americana, Prairie Schooner, Radix, Spero, Waiting and Other Poems ("A N Poetry Pamphlet," published by The Goosetree Press).

Watercolor by Margit Beck—courtesy Babcock Galle
Watercolor by Nell Blaine and oil by Hyde Solomon—courtesy Poindexter Gal
Mixed Media by Robert Rauschenberg—courtesy Leo Castelli Gal
Oil by Theodore Stamos—courtesy Andre Emmerich Gal

Distributor: USA: Folder Editions: 325 East 57th Street, N. Y. C. 22

Library of Congress Catalog Card Number: 66-20913

For Irving, Alice, and Clifford

And that your eyes come to the surface
from the deep wherein they were sunken

—*Ezra Pound*

Table of Contents

Frontispiece: Drawing: Margit Beck
Mixed Media: Robert Rauschenberg
Drawing: Elias Friedensohn
Ink and Wash Drawing: Nell Blaine
Oil: Theodore Stamos
Oil: Hyde Solomon

Book Design: Daisy Aldan
Cover: Watercolor: Margit Beck
Photography: Marlis Schwieger

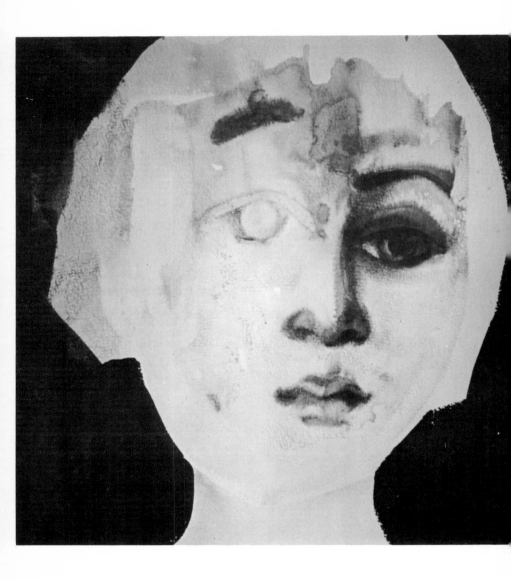

Margit Beck

Encounter

Man and bird stop suddenly.
Eye pierces eye.
One quick salute of bird to man,
a beaked and piquèd recognition.
This eye speaks not
that eye wills silences.
The moment of arrest proves vulnerable.
An alien among the trees
man seeks the shelter of his will:
but contradiction rattles him
love saddens him
fear changes him
Simplicity is sweet.
resolution forsakes him.
The bird begins to fly.
An eye for an I.
I die.

In Memory of My Sister, Nathalie Fich Oddie

(1927-1959)

Schwester, da ich dich fand an einsamer Lichtung
Des Waldes und Mittag war und gross das Schweigen des
Tiers:
—*George Trakl*

I who partake of the mundane moving in the crystals of
    morning
You who partake of the murkiness of my dreams in my
    waking hours
Along the blue fountains, through the torn weeds, in the
    seedless time,
I and you, *Schwester, da ich dich fand . . .*
If I talk with my mouth and my lips move
Your lips in my remembrance tremble in their blueness, in
    their quiver
Below those nostrils that told so much of grief.

Schwester, da ich dich fand an einsamer Lichtung
Des Waldes und Mittag war und gross das Schweigen des
Tiers:
It was my silence.

What of bone and meaning
When the flesh spent spares nothing
And the head whirls in torment
And the shreds of muscle and flower lie strewn on the grass
    and kitchen.
All, our counters of mortality . . .

You and I stand still
As the great silence
Resounds in the urn, in the subway through the open doors.
The lights in the rooms turn on;
I turn them on and leave.
Light is matter dim with fear
And with too much flesh I prefer the dark.

Schwester, da ich dich fand . . .

The animals are tigers
They ricochet in that forest
Where we surround ourselves.

Let us turn on the lights and leave.
The trees await us.

Sparrow

In the purple void
like a child flying his white kite on a coral string
flush with a telegraph pole
I stand
me with my book in hand.

Ah this perpendicular
on this vast island.

Opposite me, still, unwary,
the sparrow twits his head
and does not read
the sign
which flows from my book to him
because he has wings.
Because he has wings
he is not like the others.
So small unperceived
with a gray-brown —
prosaic bird of the day
prophet of the never-ending event
that starts and stops and starts again
without history
with only the tradition of being
his pull, his target: this barbarian.

His insouciance
my upright stance.

On the pole tantalizing alive
without the sparks that tell
here the electricity hides itself
like a sparrow's dirt-brown wing
once on the ground of stones and battered sand.

I stand
and read
the book in hand.

This telegraph pole
like the bridge
that spans an island
an island of cities
and broken territories of land
has a tensile strain.

I in my body
relent
and perform my task.
I repeat some magic words
shriek to hurl the sparrow off
and then in miscalculation
unwinged
pervious to fall
collapse
with book in hand.

Debris

What should the word be for him who has no stars?
Even my hands are not enough
and socks and shoes muddy up the waters.
When the lake is ploughed up
    and the stones removed
only the furrows will remain.

They will throw away the debris
and the voices will then hunt the song
that lame-footed thing
last seen among trees
    when the water was high and the
    nests of the birds held eggs
    instead of thistles.

Now you may take back the note.
It is hard to read the silences
and the staff sergeant has already given the
    last command of the night.

Tuck yourself in.
He may be here tomorrow.
I think he will wear white —
or at least a few bandages.
His wounds are deep.

Murder

large on the horizon
a red glowing elephant on its haunches
still silent
knowing nothing
not brooding
large bloating redness
like the red throat of a bird
thrown out in courtship
glaring
the setting sun
(fitting fire)
whole over lusts
over dead (quiet) bodies of men
miasmal
murdered men
Vietnamese

Relic

Like seaweed the white foot
lies on the sand
to be swallowed up
by the first high tide

The foam moans low
(it moans low)
and the real seaweed like jelly fish moves
nearer the foot
where now the water swirls
and toils to make more white
that pure bone

That foot
near the sea tide
must lie
dismembered
without color
with form
primordial, animal
soon to be fleshless
entire

A white clean fragment
of a man
once encumbered
by total flesh by arm
by woman
by ship's chores

by war
by a death
eccentric:

irrelevant now the womb leanings
that male body
that fatherhood
that Vietnamese whore.

Clean bone
washed by sea tide
relic

—coming from the shore
that limb once managed well
once *walked*
walked
like Him who *walked* the waves.

Electronic Music I: Sound Collage

For Robert Rauschenberg
on his "Oracle"
(with due acknowledgement to Alan Solomon's
Prolegomenon)

I must go to hear the water run
in perpetuum
those waterworks
that mobile fountain.

I must go to hear the lullaby
of that plumbing
aged with the Rauschenberg patina
or Metropolitan fallout
and gutter gangrene.

I must see a car door
cohabiting
with
a typewriter table.

I must suffer
metalwork ducting
miscegenated vehicles . . .
at last.

I must hear
five different FM frequencies
and alter
the spectrum
of sound.

I MUST HAVE INTERFERENCE
AMONG THE TRANSMITTERS

Now gently gently
I must be stable and fool-
proof.

Battery operated
connected by cables
I hear my voices.

By random tuning of the radios
(five radios
one console unit)
I make

BOOM
RATTLE
TRUMPET
GIMCRACKERY

What an antic traffic jam I am.

Electronic Music II

Splice my tape day
with the blue of the blue jay
with the blue of the blue jay
the blue of my song.

And when the noise that music makes
unstrings me
lie me low low
in my hammock marROW.

I will learn the
(yes I will)
the folk game —
the tick tack toe.

Or I will learn the
(yes I will)
the long wail — o
of the ravished
nightingale.

This is X now
and this is O.
Now
unsplice my song.

> In the anteroom
> the technician told me
> "the machine is in need of repair."
>
> (reels of tape
> unwheeled)
>
> And he told me further
> he could not program me
> no, not until,
> at least,
> the moon was in eclipse
> and the whole figuration
> of the plugs and wires
> had electronically
> produced the proper excitation.
>
> Sometimes X ➘ O.
> I responded courteously.

Electronic Music III

Notwithstanding
he placed his armor
his armorial bearings
that is his tureen
circa 1820
on the tea table

She refused to turn
being ensconced
so prettily
her toes uncovered
her shoes crossed
(a movement entrechat)
on the far settee

"Ah, mon ami," he said,
"My beautiful tureen."

She squirmed
put down her hand
to touch the arm
of the new turntable
circa 1965
to hear the
shocking
black record.

The record
e-e-led:
ting ting
          l
      e e
    w
  s

~~~~~~~~~~~~~~~~~~~~~~~~~~
\\\\\\\\\\\\\\\\\\\\\\\\\

Split spore
                    n ?
                e
              e
            r
Mag ma tu

Her toes wiggled
Her cheeks danced
Her blue eyes glistened
She turned to
his tureen.

Electronic Music IV: Accorsi's Toy
Sculpture: "The Clock"

A broom, a handkerchief
an old bead, a false moustache
a kitchen knife, some old pear seeds
a plucked out brush, a dirty comb
and one brand new Py-co-pay toothbrush
with a GIANT-SIZE Crest toothpaste:

this, this was the face
of the clock that tick-tocked
and made the boy say
WHAT TIME IS IT

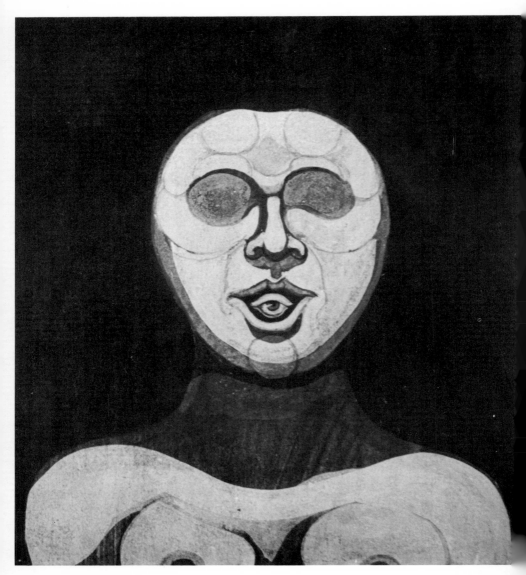

Elias Friedensohn

The Return

The roses from Pieria
and I with my hornbook of lilies

(Nothing is far-fetched
that the mind seizes upon.)

But the roses
now without stems
faded in the hands of the lady
with flax stockings, embossed,
would do well in a vase.

"It is time to put the roses in a vase," she said.
And kissing him lightly on the cheek
disposed of the lily, the book, and the stems
and faded — out.

He looked on the sofa
and saw her eyes.

"Let me pluck them," he said smiling,
plucking for each rose an eye.

"At least there are two," he said.
"Two eyes and four kisses."
"I have always been generous," he said.

Her blinded face cast down on the sofa
remained quiet now.

From Pieria two roses
from the lady two eyes.

He held the vase in his hand.
"How contented I am," he said.
Delicate, impervious eyes (his own)
cast their fondness upon eyeless woman and roses.

The camera went click

"And I am home at last."

"What a relief," the husband said.
"I thought you had gone to your lover."

Cocktail Party

Who is it stands trembling
plucking as on a violin
each sound to make it clear?
Am I calling from within?

Is this face, so unrelaxed
with smiles of courtesy or dubious chagrin
is this face another self
that holds me in?

I know that guest, lame and thin, has gone to war.
The other, who holds his face so taut,
has been to China, rather far:
I only travel as I let my door ajar.

These faces taunt me now.
My masks fall.
I am the one the other.
My fumbling will extends to each.

I hold the cocktail glass and shudder.
Will it shatter to the floor?
And shall I at home pick the pieces up —
my scattered will, the strangers' faces, the broken cup?

I flip my heart to the other side.
Is it I? Is it I?
I decide to hold the glass
and let the question ride.

the rood

he wore his cassock in the rain
(like armor)
his cold eyes shot out to the nearest tree
and withered the red ant —
it was his foot near the root
    (the splayfoot)
it was his foot near the root
would he stop in the rain
i watched him
    (behind the tree)
would he stop in the rain
in his cassock now mud upon it
when he stomped his foot
    (his splayfoot)
he got this mud
this tender mud near the ant and tree
soft splotch mud
this tender mud
upon his bod
    —y
(i saw it behind the tree)
will he go away
will he go away
i want to play
in front of the tree
the rain
it wont stop me

Blue Shirt and Portieres

He hides behind the portieres
bending down as if in whispers.
He is afraid.

The talk goes on.
The amber glasses are shadows on the floor.
The faces of the ladies pale in powder pouting into amber
are enemies.

Will they see him
hiding looking looking hiding?

His suit becomes him.
His tie tells just enough
to an observer
to enable him to move
unnoticed and befriended.

His shirt is dark blue.
The blue shirt is a boast:
"I hide here — behind the portieres.
"Come find me as I whisper to my enemies."

For the Present: Mollusks

I never see Mary in the car
(they bought it second hand)
She takes care of their infant son
who pouts in his oak crib all day

cockle shells
along the shore
(purling putrid purlieus of desire)

He walks the child by the arm
gnarled stick grasping

cockle shells
of yellow, gray, brown
(ghastly Golgotha)

At night
they examine
their collection of mollusks
their cramped tortured hearts

Duchamp's Nude Again

The sinister
    step
        down
            the
                staircase
Is
Alone
He
                Alone
Walking
    down
        the
            staircase.

Holding back the smile that burrows
(taut, beneath behind, lip concealed, teeth waiting)

He   He
is at the
    bottom of the
            stair
and then
        the floor
and then
        the door
unbolted
free him.

Into the yard of air he goes.

Air, grant him forgiveness
Street, free him from frowning
Stones, comfort him
Him (who has been walking has been talking has been
    balking)
where shoes and boots and rubbers
            have been
            have been

where dogs have sniffed
and horses have lain dead
and trolley car tracks have
and sports cars
   into the
     quiet sun

Twelve years ago he heard
   the peacocks cry
and looked upon the Indian pyramids.
In his wallet is a small stone
chiseled from a sun god
        from Kerala
twelve years ago.

Air, grant him forgiveness

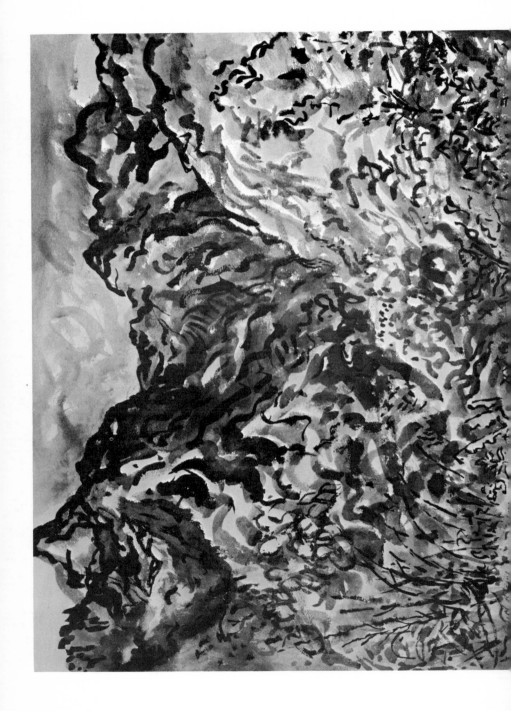

The Cat and the Stream

Now he sits beside the stream
near him a dog

At home beside the pewter jug
the cat is sleeping
and on the wormwood table
a few leaves, a water pitcher
and a cloth rumpled and old.

The stream moves him
cold as it is
with pebbles and lizards to catch the eye.

Who watches the sleeping cat now?
Is it the woman who returns to the kitchen
   for the cup
while he gazes in stupor at the silent stream?

Hide and Seek

It is not for the forsaken that the songs come to an end.
The tears in themselves are lachrymose
and the foul-mouthed lap up the obscenities.

In the wilderness the moss is unaccounted for
and in all the journeys that the weary take
the ground remains untrammeled.
    Because they do not sing.
    Because they do not weep.
    Because they do not curse.
    Because they do not kiss the grass.

High in the mountains
    the coneys hide behind the rocks
    and turn and face each other
    and turn again
    and search and search and search.

Loom Fever

Wan warp worries woof
wantonly worrying myriad wefts of loops and threads.

See where the quilt rises vermilion!

And the warp and woof weave drunkenly
over old sullen clothes
and cloths that spelled
weariness and why
and where and

Why won't you cover me?
My canvas is blood red and my soft folds
of linen ache
to be worn as
woolly weave of warp and woof.

Definitions of a Non-Empiric

FEAR

Two eyes heave out
A man groans.
Two birds fly
A feather falls.
One boy rolls one stone.

LOVE

An empty shell
Dim with sea sounds
Lies near the shore.
My fingers burn
My blood is there.

WISDOM

I love the moon
Because it is big
Because it lives in a bigger moon still
Because I am a little moon.

PROPHECY

An ant is deviously upon the floor
I watch where he is going
Where he came from I do not know
That I am here he does not know
Today we are both ignorant
Of the darker side of the moon.
Tomorrow, alas, I may not be.

Borough of Queens: Last Day of April

On that street
the house clung to the pavement
the yard was a sidewalk
the lawn
a narrow line of bushes.

Close up to the house
there was a dogwood tree
and on the broken steps
lay pink petals.

The owner of a tricycle
with the front wheel gone
made ripples in the rainwater
his face peering into the gutter.

He did not see the sun
setting near the highway
nor hear the sirens
of a city ambulance:
he was making slow circles
in his own gutter pool.

Father and Son: A Game of Catch

Stephen throws the ball.
It makes a furious arc.
Stephen pitches again.

His father ducks
catches the ball
in pain.

Drop dead!
Steve's eyes mock:
father ground grass!

The boy's cheeks are flushed.
The sun is high.
A car roars past.

Ducks in Heckscher Park

It is raining.
I walk on white lines.
Yellow circles surround me, make an arc to conform.

Quickly the rain stops.

Away they walk now,
    their beaks so yellow
        their yellow feet
            their webs.

But they have stared and stood.
    (Suddenly motionless, they wore me out.)
Their webbed feet on the white lines
    their yellow beaks thrust out.

I too stopped to stare
    at their white bodies and yellow feet.

Now I look again.
They are home on the pond.
    Yellow and white on the pond.

They turn round
    make an arc
conform.

The Sunday Outing

This baby in his carriage, tucked in,
luring the sun to keep him warm;
this father, near, washing his bright new car
(Corvette, Corvair, Grand Prix?)
(Sunday has rolled round again)
have no life on an indifferent farm
no grass and mud and chickens
no yards and baby's cries, old and lost,

but here in the flatlands of suburbia
father's eyes not knowing where
throw his love with caution —
on cleaning wax on yearning flesh

Ah, I possess you, my white Thunderbird

I seek you, my Fiat, my Sting Ray.

White carriage wheels

US RUBBER

CHROME HUBCAPS

SHH!

The cat slinks by
    stares
        jumps.

Demeter to Persephone
(For Alice)

You love *Heidi*
and the *Princess and the Pea*
and Robert Graves' *The Penny Fiddle*
and your new favorite
Jarrell's *The Bat Poet*

and you love
your little puppet
Dominique

Especially
you love
waking up
so slowly
as you circle your arms
embracing the air that you breathe

You are reborn
each morning in that slow circling
(and I
if I am lucky
sometimes see you snuggling up to that wide world)

The sun
has come up
before us
You say
the sun
and not your brother
has put that brightness in
and stirred you
to open your eyes
and circle life about

The sun
does not awaken me
it is the piercing bell
of the alarm
    and in alarm
    I jump up
        to wander
            in search of my daughter
            who has not yet tasted
            the pomegranate of Aidoneus

And this is the story
of the sun's work
I Demeter
must tell it to you
    my own Persephone

Round Head
(for Clifford)

Baby
  boy
    round head
(sometimes the round is elliptical)
like an egg)
delicate
its eyes may be round
    (or elliptical too)
but whether
always
seeing into things
this hand this bottle this self's tear

and afterwards the round ball
the square (or rectangular) chalkboard
the slender chalk

and always
the fingers
his own
to taste
  to bite
    to make a fist with

Theodore Stamos   *"Red Sun-box,"* 1965   *Courtesy Andre Emmerich (*

Waiting

He sits
single and alive
a pin pointing to no horizon
a rocket staring into space
waiting
not deciding
near a pool of water.
It is he who sits

like a rocket staring into outer space
waiting.

"It is warm-blooded," she says,
subtle, alive, waiting,
a pin pointing to no horizon
a rocket staring into space
not deciding
waiting
near a pool of water
where a. fish swimming
around around
makes a tiny whirlpool
waiting
in the cold.

"It is fearless," she says,
she, dancing,
a sun beating down
her shadow on empty waters.

Word As Gesture

This simple word rests flat on the page.
Page reads the word back to me.
As it rests, I rest.
Both, in the oblivion of having been,
having been expressed.

What simple gesture
do I now demand
when the ink runs dry
and the boat sinks beneath the water
and the smile submerges in the tomb
and the weak voice utters that last cry,
I have been.
I die.

That silent stone
that block of time
the immemorial gesture of
I have been.
I die.

Definitions

Definitions like petals fall asleep.
If I wonder how the mind conceives
or labors at inconceivables
If I seek to fathom what concept is
what concept can and cannot stir the mind
If I probe what notions to me deride
the notion of myself
myself and you and immortality
If I think
I am bemused
and the mind in me
that you engendered sharp and clear
is dull and flat.
It seeks your definition.

Let your will define me.

and the fruit

"... if you say *apple* to a modern critic you will be pelted
with religion, mythology, and Freud before you can duck."
—Karl Shapiro

     APPLE

A
  P
    P
      L
       E

a
  P
    P
      l
       e

     APPLE

apple

"apple"

"APPLE"

a p p l e

(*is* in the midst of the garden)

red
  round
    stem

(eaten)

"the edible fruit, usually round and red, of a
  rosaceous tree
    Malus pumila (pyrus Malus)"

i want to eat you

(*was* good for food)
ab ovo usque ad mala
red
  (*was* pleasant to the eyes)
  round
    green stem
      (usually withered, to brown)

i want to eat you
i want to eat you
(a petty Trespass)
are you there
Io
answer me
(to make me wise)
Bacche
pyrus malus
my pyre will be re
dripping rotting p
circumstantial evi
O O O O O O O

Turquoise

Turquoise?
Who?
Are you?
I look: the *t* the *u* and the *r*
the *q* I squeeze tight
out of reason
the *u* again makes me mindless
the *o* and the *i* go together
and I am headachy
se are the beauties of the word
I look and sleep
peacefully

In my dream
plankton
phos phor es cence
blue-green
seaweed
and deep in ocean beds
the call
ultramarine
deep-sea mollusks
an abyssal world I take home with me

a gay time was had by the pig whose pen bled

anemone
dahlia
cicada
coup

trianon
mischief
palindrome
shoe

heart
ankle
burr
knee

trumpet
tulip
turkey
tea

slop is the fashion

"It Is Well Known"

"It is well known."
"It is dangerous."
"Temptation is irresistible."

> The center holds the black round eye.

"The path is hard."
"Error is everywhere."

> The canvas is light blue.

Who torments the child with the McGuffey Reader
and tears the canvas at its black throbbing center?

> The page is white
> and the President is dead

He Speaks

Below the burrowing Bosporus
betwixt between betrothed
the tawny furbelow tirade
bespeaks my true-love loth.

Bespeak the bones below the boss
beturn betwist bespoken:
"Be sure the door is barred belocked;
"be sure it is not broken."

O well the whirling welkin woes
O what wherefore beehive?
O slowly sloughs the slovenly:
"Comtesse—control, contrive."

Hyde Solomon   *"Horizon"*   *Courtesy Poindexter G*

Beyond the City

Beyond the city
    (near the swamps)
when the wind comes slowly
there is no reed that is quiet

King Midas Has Ass's Ears

Even to bathe in the springs of the Pactolus
                          (near Mt. Tmolus)
has its dangers
and a Phyrgian cap hides nothing from one's barber

So the pursuit of men
the ravages
through whispers

Food in the hand is a nugget in the mouth
gold in sand glimmers and kills
the heart lies quiet but once

Dog Days

if you should discard it
the loss of it
the where will it be
under the stone step
here near the bush
where only the dog goes
the loss of it
will discover it for you

you will begin
that brown leaf will point the way
you will feel
a remissness?
yes
such careworn tapestry look in your heart
you will follow
the dog himself
you will sniff

sniff your way
behind the stone step

I see you now
old with a whiff of hair
sitting on the stone step
sniffing

. . . such dog days
there are
in store for you

Burning

What youth
from the flames of Phlegethon
will rescue his bride

Once he turns his back
the funeral pyre burns
though the screams reach heaven

Chantons

I will not for your displeasure
crunch this daw-diver
down that River Styx
toward that pathway.

He that went the dog-eared moon along
and with a partner in the enterprise
sought a mate in those crevasses;
I saw you to go
to bypass that transaction.

What the will wishes
the lunar path pushes
toward.

Only the circumstances change.
You do not have to mind that.
This path, that one.
One long river edge is as good as another —

if it throbs throbs
that cool water
au clair de la lune.

To Margit: Green Leaf In Your Studio

How surprised you were
that the leaf
in December
pushed
violently in —
through the window
unannounced
a hothouse guest
in your
acrylic garden

Stoned

The snails keep pace with me
and the pebbles on the ground
are white, black, gray, purple, even orange.

The pebbles are homes for snails
nests for the water snakes
leaping laps for lizards.

I have been stoned
by the rocks
far away from the pebbles.

Below those ravines
the beavers find the rocks.
The logs cover them well.
But not enough to hide them.

The agony of that pain!
The bearing up under it!

Stoned and snailed.
Paced and pounded.

Remnant

Look at that world, the finger nail,
a remnant, bitten off, lying on the table.
A pale moon, unmoved,
fallen, disparate, unstable.

The wind has scattered the feather of a bird,
disconsolate thing.
My nail is equally unfurbished.
(A bit sordid, that is true,
as any castoff is.)

In the end neither will do.
A nail without a finger tip lies
wasted. The feather without the bird
never flies.

But I'll bite my nail
to replenish myself
by a process of attrition:
and birds will fly.

An Aged Man Is But a Paltry Thing

Does he stare into the air
because he feels he is not free
to die?

He who has no son
has not won
his freedom.
Where will he search
in this age
for woman to bear him one?

He is alone
because woman
has betrayed him.
(By whose plan
was he left
so bereft?)

She has left him whole.
He has won
no son.
All in one
he is heir and father
he who cannot be supplanted.

Shoebox

Here I am
an old woman
living in a shoe
(my heartbeat, and all my toes
and that sunk-in feeling through and through).

This shoe
I keep in the closet
in a box
with tissue paper.

(I take care
it receives
no uncertain wear
no feet with the ague
no beat abnormally askew.)

Who should see it
Who should free it
from the box
and the paper?

Maybe it will be
you

but do you
have so many children
you don't know what to do?

On the Mountain

Has the old lady died?
Did she succumb to that cruel heart?
Or is the hearse waiting waiting to pick up an
    undertaker for other doors?
Yes, its business is yet to be done.

The lawn, I see, is still well kept.
The rocks that have lain dead for centuries
have not been removed.

But where is the body?
Will it be driven down the valley soon?
I see the blinds of the hearse are drawn
But the driver's seat is empty
And the door of the house remains shut.

Desolate house on the mountain
Why is there a hearse in front of your door?

Cybelean Matters

I shall return to the earth, the primordial
me Gaea, crest'fallen Christ leaning
space injecting the firmament
while Uranus leaps and warms the giants' home
Tell us tell us tell us.

There in the rush of waters drying
and red rot roasting and the conflagration
to ease chaos of pain the landlubber wooed
strange beatitude, Cybele, the young-old.
Tell us tell us tell us.

(All the old curses)
The infant waxeth green
Tell us tell us tell us.
Whoa whoa the wind whiles away
oh no oh no say
who lured largesse to the giants' den?
Tell us tell us tell us.

Gravida gravida gravida
Tell us tell us tell us.

Cityscape

Listening to the twittering
    of the airconditioner
wondering about
    sand dunes and sea gulls
    and the waves' white foam
I am wooed
by the silence
of my mind's
murmurings.

How shall I be restored.?
I cannot go down
    to the sea again
nor can I
whittle the wood birds
of my beginnings.

The birds I see
on my mantelpiece
are stone
sculptured
free of the hand
that made them

and the waters of my mind
ebb
    and flow
to the distractions
    of my only source
that thing
    in early days
I called my heart.

The sound
of the airconditioner
has stopped

but my mind
    goes on
    to birds again
to the waves' white foam
    and the dreary business
of reaching
    a distant shore.

If the lighthouse
        beams
I used to see
        on that far island
could flicker now
I might be tempted
to risk
        the world of the sea again.
to watch
        the sea gulls waiting
        standing erect
        on the grassy dunes.

But it is summer
in the city
among airconditioners
and doormen's whistles

and the people
wear a bold tan.

They have grabbed
the sun
in the way they can.

I must worship
at the sun a while
        on my terrace
                above the city street
before the sun
        goes down.

Blue Wings

Blue wings white breast
master me
Bare branch
smothers me
Wings fly high
I lie
at the foot of the tree.

Resembling me
the leaf unstemmed
waits on the ground
and the snow
covers the grass
where squirrels pass
unwittingly

The road nearby
circles the tree
No one walks
No one sees
that blue winged bird
that dormant me
lying beneath that tree

The sun appears
The bird flies
one branch the other
indifferently
The sun goes down
The sky flies
over me

MEn

Me. And me now.

—*James Joyce*

MEn . . . the nEM
esis
of dreams,
to placate destiny
and throw the body to Scylla
and the EM
blEM of the naMEless
to Charybdis
fog mist wind . . .
have chosen well.

CoME.
There within the forest
is the egg
still
formidable
a MEre shell
lying waiting
to be gobbled up
to be eaten
by MEmory.

MEntion this to no man.
He knows the secret
(and can dEMonstrate it
to the wide world
unerringly).

The Word

Bulges of lips on the page —
words are not enough
(as any poet knows)
and lips move
and even if nothing is said
there is the motion
and the pretense.

Rather masks of lips
than meaninglessness.

Protruding lips
on the very margin of the page.
Let someone draw them
paste them
(open and shut)
distinctly
in red.

Script and type and lips
mechanisms.
Only the lips mercurial
tell more . . .

I didn't hear you.
What did you say?

Marvels on the page
are not marvels
without a reader.

"No action upon an object
without retroaction of that object
upon the subject."
But the lips move
and stare
palpable object
itself subject
seeking the source
with readying kisses
always there

more source
than printed word
in itself the thing
and image too;
being
incurring within itself
stance and passion
reflecting to itself
other passions other mouths

always emitting
worthy of saliva
of pear and peach
of yesterday's oatmeal
today's steak
tomorrow's vinaigrette

worthy of sores and blisters
of rugged (red) chappedness
of the tears
from eyes its own face possesses.

Better tears from eyes
than printed rhetoric.

Or is sometimes
a word remembered
as if it had a life of its own?

No. A word is from an alphabet
already lost abandoned
devised out of need
utilized until meaningless.

That word remembered
is death
a verbal corpse.
It belonged to another age
had another meaning
and no ambiguity
can replace
the fleshliness
embodied in its own
first echo.

The word can only be denied.

In the beginning was the word
the word was made flesh
let the words of my mouth ... be acceptable.

The word is gone out of my mouth ...

AN EYE FOR AN I has been set in Garamond type
and printed on laid paper. A limited number
of copies is available in hard cover and numbered.

Printing by The Pierson Press
New York City